For Luck: Poems 1962-1977

Books by H. L. Van Brunt

Uncertainties (1968)

Indian Territory and Other Poems (1974)

Feral: Crow-Breath and Caw (1976)

For Luck: Poems 1962-1977 (1977)

H. L. Van Brunt

For Luck: Poems 1962-1977

Carnegie-Mellon University Press

Pittsburgh & London 1977

Acknowledgments

8/1978
Am. Lit.

PS
3572
A42
F6

The author wishes to thank Eleanor Torrey West of the Ossabaw Island Project and Mary Nikas of the Jay Hambidge Art Foundation for residence fellowships that enabled him to complete this book

The poems in this book first appeared in the following publications:
The Smith, Foxfire, Bitterroot, The Literary Review, Midwestern University Quarterly, Writings, Red Clay Reader, Gnosis, Quartet, Lynx, Meanjin Quarterly, Tulsa Poetry Quarterly, Poet Lore, Icarus, Per/Se, Hearse, Southwest Review, Red Cedar Review, Arlington Quarterly, South Dakota Review, Kansas City Star, Twigs, Latitudes, The Unspeakable Visions of the Individual, West Coast Review, New Orleans Review, The New York Times, Kansas City Times, December, The Arts in Ireland, Nimrod, Cimarron Review, Hampden-Sydney Poetry Review, Three Rivers Poetry Journal, Poetry NOW, Confrontation, The Sole Proprietor, The Nation, New Letters, The American Poetry Review

for the Grandmothers and the Grandfathers

Rebecca Tucker   Robert E. Lee Johnson
Esther Perkins   Peter Van Brunt

and for Laura

Contents

II. from *Indian Territory and Other Poems*

From
Uncertainties

FOR WILLIAM FAULKNER

With the silent, grim
bleak quality of truth
he changed into earth.

An instrument
sixty years in the making
quit working,

its insides rusted out.
The corpse was scrapped
in the usual manner:

melted down
in the furnace of a grave.
His ashes feed the roots —

he is
the tree
they buried him by.

EMBERS

An old woman
with eyes like wasps' nests
turns from a path on to
the graveled road.

Sheaved in rags
she walks the dawn home,
haggling
with low embers in the sky.

STRANGERS

They stop by the river, northward here,
leaning in their saddles —
ponderous men who strayed here and there
for a while, on their journey.

The heads of their horses toss and jangle.
The heavy men wait, while slow
repetition of breath brings dreaming
of no new place to go.

THERE IS

There is only
dust
and darkness
on this road.
Memory chews
the yellowed crusts
of years.
Tonight the stars —
white buffalo —
graze in deep
pastures.

SHADOWS

There was the wind at nightfall,
hills, prairie turning grey;
the woods in the river bottom,
odour of water and stars;
the entreaty of night:
stay here, the world is light.

Light there was, inside the screen door
where my mother leaned
peering into the darkness
before she decided
to call.
There was a light in every room.

She never understood
why I didn't come.

THE HUNTERS

We saw a wolf
that saw us first.
Wind dipped from
trees to snow.
We had a way to go.

My stepfather's .22
looked like an elephant
gun. My rifle shot a cork.
He walked as sure as an Indian,
avoiding the drifts and thinner ice.

I floundered on behind.
Stumbling out of those blackjack woods
I was first to my uncle's house.
We had a fight. I shot him twice
before we had to go.

The night was mostly moon and snow.
He was cross: not a thing to shoot
at but that wolf all day.
And he had missed.
I howled the long way home.

IN SELF-DEFENSE

I shot birds in self-defense
when I was fourteen with a .22.
I killed them while they sang.

Later, tossing their shocked bodies
in the brush, or seeing them drift
away on the current of the creek,

I never thought they were kin to me —
as I stood secure in another dimension,
as ignorant of wrong as right.

Now I know death in any direction
comes without the aid of a .22,
and feel no joy over crumpled bodies

or exultation at blood's flow.
And know myself, as I remember
beating to death a rabbit in the snow.

THE EVENT OF MY GRANDMOTHER'S DEATH

1.
Dawn was the usual
darkness fading.
The scalpel of the sun
lay bare
earth's skeleton.
Birds did not
record the day
in flight or song.
The river flowed
as always before.
Wind cracked the flag like a whip, and seemed
to smell of rain.
The sun edged on beyond high clouds.

2.
She lay in her plush casket
the way she had been put
by undertaker's grace.

Those who knew they loved her
(one then two then three)
didn't bother to wait

for the eulogy.
Nor did they attend
the second ceremony

to hear the minister
and funeral director
discuss the trade and weather.

Instead, they had a drink,
then two, then three, then four —
then more.

3.
A rug of paper grass
lay over the mounded grave.
Rain still thinly fell,
gauzing the leafy trees.
We stood drunk as we were
and silently cursed
all the things
we cannot change.

THE OLLOGAH DAM

1.
The black elm was all there was.
The one that always sprouted
Those pale, stillborn buds
That stank and littered the yard.

The creek which ran so clear
At the bottom of the hill
Was a slough of mud and boulders
The state would slowly fill.

Bulldozers on the edge
Of the cliff seemed huge grasshoppers
That had ravaged the bottom woods.
The bald prairie where the moon

Flooded white and full
Above the knoll, the wild hay
Inhabited by wind,
The pumphouse whose metronome

Was the heartbeat of the land,
Were gone —
There was only a flat
Morass charred black.

2.
The water has slowly backed
Up to the very foundation
Of the house I helped to build
When I was six years old.

My friends have snagged their lines
On stumps of trees I climbed.
Wind pushes from the west.
The moonfaced water laps.

BEYOND THE SURF

Storms are leveling somewhere.
But here things go from side to side.
Old women of my sleep

rise to stir the coals.
But I will not
be kept awake.

In the house at the back of my head
I am secure.
Winds can't reach me there.

I am floating on my back
beyond the surf
on the morning of a dream.

A FLOWER FROM THE SEA

The sea makes the same old sounds
And slaps the sand and slides.
Slowly she is pushed in

By waves that break and glide.
Her hair floats long and blonde.
She stares at the blue-white sky.

Her skin is peeling off.
What's left of her has changed —
Dumped upon the sand.

NEAR THE END

We stood and watched the water
wash over, spray sea boulders
that seemed great tidal trees
burned black by ocean fire.
The air was heavy with the surge
and din of all that water.
We sucked in breaths and sighed them out,
wishing we were of
the league of rocks and trees and sky
and moss and fern —
rooted in earth or sea.
But behind us lay the path
that we had climbed so long,
and the setting sun.
We stood beneath the embers
of another day.
Before us lay the dark
rocks and sea.

DRIVING TO CHICAGO

I remember the plains
south of Chicago.
The plowed earth spread over the horizon.
That horizon glowing
as dusk fell like a mist.

There can't be a real
city around here, I said as we were passing
weedy private airports
with their dinky private planes —
thinking surely to find another
place with a dozen stoplights
and one cop parked under a tree.
But already we were there,
in a pall of neon signs,
fenced factories with dumpy yards,
smoke, and railroad tracks.

We smoothly ascended whatever it was —
skyway, freeway — anyway the city
flowed beneath us like a river
of broken walls and chimney pots.

Our room was high and hygienic.
We unpacked, we ate, after walking an hour
in the Loop, we even made love
(hotel rooms always excited you).
Then slept. I woke. It was 3:00 A.M.

I thought through the morning of the night
how close the stars were to the prairie
in Oklahoma, the sound the wind made
when we stopped to stretch
(how I would like to own that farmhouse
if you would stay there with me)
in southern Illinois.

SUNLIGHT

A needle's point
(in the dark of the
room
where two cigarettes
oranged and subsided
in sweaty fingers) was
the speck in your eye
when I turned
my head.

Blonde sunlight, you later said,
was the better companion
for your head.
I didn't argue, though
I might have had an urge
to try to explain
how little
sunlight you
had seen.

AN ELEGY

Serenity infinite as space
Basks in the evening sun.
The idiot's face
As he twirls a toy
Moonward lists to sunward —
Eyes like messages
In bottles put out to sea.

I have found what I was looking for,
Walking through this evening,
Jumbling our last conversation —
As a leaf beneath the glass
Magnifies and burns
So the seasons of our lives
Consume themselves.

THE RAGPICKER

One morning when you hear a wheel
grating over the street
you'll open your window
and see an old man
pushing a cart.
As he trundles by,
just before he turns
the corner,
you'll see, heaped high,
every garment
you have worn.

STAGES

In the quiet
enveloping of a night
when something rises
and seems to light the sky,
and when that flare subsides
and I am alone again
with that quiet that is quieter than before —
when all sound has been rescinded
and there is nothing
but far-off shapes like mountains
that are bigger than before —
I ask myself
how could I have come
to this
not caring —
this only
vaguely resenting
my own dying.

FOOTSTEPS

Footsteps on the stair —
from the bottom of the well
the footfalls of my fear
climb and, climbing, bear
the world of my hell —
greetings from everywhere.

The semi-summered air
of cooking smells and dog
urine and the hot
tar of melted streets . . .
I wind down in the sheets.
The fan blows cool and bare;

and winter's in my head.
But I must rise; another
summer morning's
unconscious thoughts come to —
I must rise and make the old
of my existence new.

TOWARD THE CENTER

Paying no attention
to star-like clusters
of hanging leaves and stems
I dive headlong
into the massive
center of the dark.
But where the trunk was
there is nothing —
the tree that rose before me and seemed
the growth of my own life
has receded
till there is nothing, nothing, nothing —
headache on the ground.

COUNT THE DEAD

The old magnificat is gone
    save where the dying
        brush the coals
            away from whitened lips.

I could count the stars, and miss
        the dead
    where stars are dying —
see the blue fade down the dark
    where the live are lying.

Miss me, count me among
        the lampposts
    on summer evenings
in small towns where moths make noise
    and wind plays in the dust.

I walk between the roses
        massed on either side
    beneath a nave of sky
singing the canticle of my life —
    lost in the motion of the clouds
        rising with the sun.

TODAY IN AUGUST

All the trees today stand quick with birds,
sitting, shitting, screwing, singing,
knitting with the flashing needles of their flights
the whole fabric of their lives.

And trees, they are as green
as algae — spongy looking,
as if each could hold
a whole skyful of rain.

I could drink
a whole skyful of rain,
munch on the trees
and make a pie of all the birds.

I feel so holy
this August day
I could eat the world.
And if I were God I would.

THE SILENCE

The faceless man, who leans his head
over an iron parapet
at dusk in an older section of the city,
lowers his eyes into the river and himself.

He stares at the last arc of sun, and voices
break the street into a pattern of cries,
assertive and threatening —
the howl of another world.

IN THE OSTERREICH

Gliding on the rim
of darkness, like a jellyfish,
the moon blurs, then dims

as it sinks into the ocean of the sky.
I have seen moon photographs:
a hulk, half-dark, and dry.

The rain with dirty fingers
streaks the grimy street.
The puzzle of the night

lies scattered by the wind.
And I, a Humpty Dumpty
who never saw a king,

lie waiting for
whatever
will put me together again.

From
Indian Territory AND OTHER POEMS

Indian Territory

BLOOD OF THE LAMB

1.
i see you
sister said
tongue consistency of a cat's

watching me come all over
some technicolored
ass

my sister's mouth would have held the moon
her eyes
were innocent as doris day's

("my hair's
as blonde
as hers")

2.
my family have died like poets for generations
moving to their own rhythm
new york to tennessee

tennessee to oklahoma
farmers, carpenters, whisky-makers
liars, thieves & soldiers

bad lungs & pride
in a queer dutch name
their only legacy

bragging they were barons of new york
when the puritans slept
with the indians

3.
my sister died
coughing & laughing & smoking lucky strikes
in a hospital on the prairie

DEATH OF THE INDIAN CARPENTER

the timber rattler's head
swung heavy as a plumb
into your log-thigh

. . . .

the buck you didn't kill
beds down on a rise

warm breath, and belly full
as the harvest moon
that's red on the window

of the tahlequah funeral home
& shines in his eyes

ON THE PRAIRIE

The house leans back
like an old man
fallen asleep in the waning sun.
A porch plank lifts
a rusty nail.

No one lives here now.
No other house for miles.
Nothing but yellow grass
and sandstone,
keeping quail company.

LION

Old man, your face is like the moon's
topography — valleys, mountains, rivers
cracked and dry.
The side you never show
darkens in your eyes.

In the cave of this old house
your room's the den you'll die in.

Smelling of Vaseline
your life's compressed
to rags of memory.
They'll sweep you out with the dust —
wrapped in Police Gazettes.

THE SPRING

The sky wore clouds
the way the marshal
wore his hat.
He kept telling us that
we'd like it there.
Movies twice a week,
and school
right on the premises.
His eyes were hidden as the sun.
The highway ran through the trees like a trail.

My sisters always liked the spring.
They built their dollhouse there.
The black
water spilled
into the creek
by its own weight.
We sat on the leaves like Indians,
tossing pebbles at the waterbugs.

They sat us down in a room like a shed.
The woman urging us to eat
was big as a house, or a hall, or the world
that placed us there. But in our eyes
she disappeared.

I hardly write to my sisters now.
They remind me of the matron
that slapped us till we ate.

Only the one who died has eyes
the color of the spring,
and arms loose as leaves.

RUNNING TOWARD THE SUN

you kindle my sleep
O enormous eyes
in a small ship's frame
I touch your heart
you die

Yes, I will take care of my brother.
(Remember I memorized the Bible,
was called to recite verses in front of the class,
and stood bewildered and hated and wondered
what was wrong.)
I promise you that.
Please sleep
in your dirt bed.

O you who never relented
who never gave anything up to the world
your small fists
failed

Elva, Elva, Cherokee-Swede
Doomsayers all
haunting the grave
as though they had never been alive

Alive to see a girl walk over the grass
twenty summers ago — flower-frail.
I'll take my children back, you said.
We ran toward the sun,
away from matrons, and the mass
of the unloved, and orbited.

But O we let you go.
We saw your suffering as a sign . . .
or curse on us, and cursed you for it.
We lived in the real world
where love doesn't cure anything at all,
where staring children swear to get even
for everything you couldn't give.

And who let you die alone.
Who wears the emblems of the sun.
And who will die himself alone
as a young or an old unlovely man —
crying for his mother,
and love that does not return.

ON THE DEATH OF C. B. REYNOLDS

Something fumbles at the latch.
The sleeping man yells *hey! hey! hey!*
Over and over —
Flopping like a fish
In a huge palm.

I remember you for what you weren't.
How easily authority sat upon you —
The sense of a man who knew his place —
And with what rightful wrath
Authority came down.

I wonder if you went down to death
With the same sense of place.
If, for a moment, you lost trust
In the ways of the Lord.
Certainly you admitted they were strange.

Charles Bryan Reynolds, I could say
You had been conned, and put upon
All of your natural life —
That the men you idolized
Shat in much the same way as you —

That dreams you had (finding gold
On that old farm; becoming an actor . . .
From usher at the Wichita Paramount;
Finding Valhalla in New Mexico)
Were cheap, not worthy of your soul.

But you were selfish. You reserved
The best you had for your own senses.
The leanest porkchop, the biggest eggs
Went on your plate. Humbly we watched
You deliberate.

"Spell 'black,' " you said; I couldn't; watched
You down in wolfish bites my cake.
"B-l-a-c-k," you said.
Turning to mother,
"He don't seem so smart to me."

Always that set of horseteeth taunted:
"Don't fall down — Mama'll cry."
"Blockhead" was the favorite epithet
You spat, and the bedsprings creaked a little louder
Nights after days we had arguments.

Charles Bryan Reynolds — Born, August, 1899,
Indian Territory. Dead, April, 1969,
The New Orleans Veterans Hospital,
Of tuberculosis — following mother
By a year — I wish you well.

And ask your forgiveness of my hate;
And for not wanting to be an actor
Or dreaming of New Mexico
I offer this, to expiate:
To mine the gold on the farm of my father.

THE HOMECOMING

Fires on the mountains,
night winds, the drift of seas
are all the same to me —
my home is in my head.

Grass and earth report
nothing I do not know —
not dissonance of trees,
or semaphores of snow.

Whales going home
follow in my wake.
Venus charts our courses.
We move for our own sakes.

Journeys never ending,
lives never begun
relate themselves as wind
and prairie grass become

a hymn in praise of nothing
. . . the way
things work under the sun.
We are like the clouds,

that change from sky to sea.
It is, as I have said,
all the same to me.
My home is in my head.

MORNING

nothing is more silent than a star
except a heron
standing at the water's edge
neck cocked like a gun

JOURNEYS

The conversations of the leaves
Turn to silence on the river,
And in that silence reigns the sun,
And in those legions of the leaves,
As they strike against their neighbors,
The wind sows the secrets of the sun.
In several tongues and several voices
Leaf-choirs begin to separate,
Their deaths now individual
As they journey to the woods
That lie in the next world.

DROWNING

placing stones sweet as chocolates
on the graves of emperors
i move

my hands through the light
bridges
to the dark below

one-half of me is black
and one-half white
i hold

the water to my breast
as though it were the child
of my life

BIRDS IN HAND

You seem to recede when you go to sleep.
Something about you evades the light.
When I cup your hips in my hands
I am entering the world.

They say you are cold, but I don't believe it.
That's just your way of being polite.
You tell men what you think of them in bed —
Where it counts, and doesn't have to be said.

Your body speaks many languages.
Lips proclaim your liberality.
And I sing like a bird
In the foliage of your limbs.

A WALK BEFORE DINNER

Something drops out of the leaves
on something else.
Owl on fieldmouse.

I do not even hear the small scream
or the heavy wings beat back to the tree,
or fix the position of the moon

above the dark cloudbanks.
But walk the river, where luminous rafts
of mosquitoes float silently by,

and tree shadows hang in the water.
Smoking, I hear
an occasional fish

splash.
But mostly the quiet air breathes
on my cheek,

and makes me hungry.
My wife should have on the table
the old hen whose neck I wrung today.

GOING HOME

My line is lifted
from the water
by an evening breeze.
Darkness walks
along the river
like the shadow
of a man.

I have caught
carp all day.
No bass, no catfish,
no large perch.
Some thoughts of you.
I shall loose the carp
to their dark home.

MELTING

The moon breaks
through the window
of this greenhouse

called a room.
Tendrils drag
across my face.

Night
is a pimp with wornout whores
that I have slept with countless times.

The bare tree
rises, with the wind
for leaves.

The moon,
confessor to the night,
is near and far

as God. Murders
break out of my head.
Asleep

I rape the world.
I have forgotten
everything I learned.

THE CITIZEN

So, of course, being law-abiding,
recently moved from the country, and awed
by the machinery of the government
I even helped them lift the dog
into the van —
saw him cower
and look down
(who had only held the arm
of some kid who hit my sister).

Now, of course, I'm full of theories —
discussing Hegel, literature,
revolution, Che Guevara —
but in my gut I know I am
that ignorant, sixteen-year-old coward,
too dumb to know of licenses,
who helped a bunch of
sons-of-bitches
murder what he loved.

The City, The Sea & The World

A CHRISTMAS POEM

A woman staggers along the street,
talking to everyone she meets,
trying to explain her life.
Now she is pulling off her clothes,
but no one bothers to listen
even to this baring
of her soul.

She will wake in jail,
and add another blotch to the spreading
                              bruise that is her life.

Haze has settled on the city.
Sunday morning
turns in the distant sky.
All human blood revives
to sing hosannas to the sun —
in whose light it gushes, with good cheer,
from our images.

LEGEND

clouds like long, black veils
bandage the sky

the river's so black tonight
the dead must get lost

perhaps they sit like owls
huddled in the trees

that run in lines across the city
waiting for the sky to clear

MINSTREL

in the nest of his shoulders rode
toucans, parrots, and a hummingbird
trilling out his life
in arias of alcohol

the cave of his stomach was filled with the small
bones of women
the green
edges of his head had turned to cheese

blue tide rising from the edge of the sea
birds that gather
in the skies
listen to me

he did not like to touch dead things
or fill his mouth with shadows
but wanted the red flag of his tongue to fly
over meadows

and hold what he held dear beside him
and listen to the words of water and wind
blades of grass were his cold children
but you were indifferent as his eyes

that faced the grey faces of the streets
and flew no flags but those of wine
a bottle smashed in either hand
as he was hit   now sing GODDAMN!

WALKING

I sing the body electric . . . — Whitman

Trees with
leaves of rain
shine
down long rows of streets.
Footsteps pound. From heels a curious
surging of the nerves
floods in steady shocks. Hands
feel electric. Eyes
glow more than a cat's. Body,
organic as a tree,
with perfect faith in molecules,
would walk to the end of the world —
singing blood's syllables.

CHINA BLUE

for Laura

Clouds like
bruises bloom
on the sea at Montauk.

Today was china blue.
Clouds became the sand
between our toes.

We stared,
our lives like the days of wasps
without a nest.

We stared,
our lives
larval in the sea.

THE GOD THAT GOES WITH THE WIND

There is a blue horizon always
rising from the sea,
and a ship that is growing smaller,
disappearing into the sky,
and a gull
rising and falling
as waves rise and fall —
isolate, priestly,
as though attending
the God that goes with the wind.

The image is that of a man
going out of himself —
the ship bearing his body always ahead
while his mind returns to where he has been
and his heart follows the wind.

THE BURGLAR

for Laura

the squawking, whining, scraping
breakfast of the gulls

startles you to waken
slide from the cocoon

of covers, gold and naked
shivering in the barred

sunlight through the window
you ask what that was

the roof is a boneyard
i say, our friends, the gulls

use it to crack the skulls
of clams, crabs, and snails

i thought it was a burglar
you say, i said it was

PETRELS

they look like the birds
that service crocodiles

picking the sea's
enormous teeth

dust the waves
like butterflies

cut
blue dolls out of the air

their voices hardly
sound like the rain

more like crows
that catch the rain in their throats

THE FORAGERS

Gulls have necks that move like worms
through the body of the air.

Balanced wings powered
by engines of the wind
they veer the wake for hours —

treasure-hunting garbage
dumped from the stern.

They prefer, as we, the visible —
the placenta of a ship
they gobble in the wake

to the fierce & picturesque
pursuit of silver fish.

THE HEIR

I have seen the moon
hanging like a windbell
from the tallest tree in Tulsa.
The stars howled all night long.
The baby drags his diaper on the ground.
"What's there you like
about New York?
Jesus. . . the smell's enough. . . "
A girlfriend moaned in the backseat —
gnashing her teeth in the insulated dark
while dreams flew in and out of trees like bats.
The baby nags her breasts
that, loosened, protrude like hills
with blue trails.

. . . .

"Jack's so much better-natured, now —
wait'll you see him!"
I see
the sores on the face of a child in Tangier
as I watch your baby suck, his cheeks
soft as the pouches of a squirrel —
eyes closed, like doors
to the throneroom of the world.

MEMOIRS

The trees in deserted Paris
On the Boulevard St. Germain
Stand recessed like huge vaginas
Sucking the August air.

O, all the *Parisiens* go down
Along the Mediterranean.
Then the *concierge* adores
Even *L'Americains*

(Vulgar as they are).
Comment allez-vous, Monsieur?
Très bien, we said, we said
Before we fled to bed —

That was so huge we both got lost
And never quite recovered.
I wonder if that bed still stands
With the *bidet* in the corner.

They seem so sensible, that race.
One can clean one's ass with grace
Before commenting on the worth
Of all the masters in the Louvre.

"Damned Frogs," we heard one jolly fellow
Say to his wife whose name was Mabel,
"Let's get the hell back to Alabama!"
We wished them well, and sat down at a table.

There is nothing like the breeze
That floats across the Seine
When you are sitting with your girl
And know it's going to rain.

Paris, I could write you our memoirs.
We no longer live together.
And when we try we can't quite ever
Separate the sweet from bitter.

So let us look through the *Bois de Boulogne,*
L'Orangerie, and the *Cimetière*
For two who simply loved one another.
They are there.

WAITING

1

The wet wind wore us down,
shaggy clouds
scratching the sides of mountains,
flooding the Attersee —
clouds we watched
through the afternoon
when all we had to smoke was kef,
all to eat, sardines, and screwed,
and laughed at the old woman
listening in the next room —
clouds that ran like a pack of mongrels,
licking the marrow from our bones
noon after afternoon.

2

Nursing beers, we watched the workmen
drink May wine. With lifted voices
they sang what seemed to us school songs,
goosing one another between choruses;
growing sad at last.

3

When you came off the last bus from Salzburg
after three days. . . I couldn't speak
but nearly broke your back. You threw
yourself and all that lovely money
all over the bed. You were like my mother
twenty years before at the orphans home —
come back from the dead.

4

I'm sure those packs of clouds still run
over the mountains of the Attersee —
the water turning before the wind
blue and black and grey;
and in the yard our room looked over
the same old pregnant apple tree
drops its hard green bastards down.

DECEMBER LETTER TO NINA

The Negro in my old room is sick
With the flu. I have it too.
Where did you say you were going to go?

They have called the Department of Public Health
Who advise that he don his uniform
Or the Doctor will not come.

Let's see, you said you would be back
Tomorrow — or was it the other day?
I am to meet you going the other way.

The hotel in Salzburg is cold. They want
The rent, and threaten to call the police.
You must be in line at American Express.

We don't spend *too* much time together.
It must be the Negro, or the Doctor.
What did you say that was the matter?

. . . .

The weather's getting cold. Snow
piled up to the windowsill. I sit
and brood on what I know.

SNAPSHOT

Cradling the Greek
    fisherman's sweater
as though it were a child, you sit
    surrounded by Dubrovnik.

The bay
    flows through your eyes.
Mountains
    grow out of your head.

You watch
    a few goats
herded by a crone
    straggle up the road.

You felt
    only disgust,
you said.
    The foetus was a mess.

LAKE/MAN/BIRD

a sudden current
of air through reeds
and there it is
the lake   all alone
a huge belly of grey water
dawn

one thing receding before the next
hill on mountain   peak on peak
bird on the water   what
does that feeble
high-pitched cry
have to do with your life

this is all you will ever have
dawn   grey water   a lone swan
swimming in circles
feathers grey
as an old man's hair. . .

POEM FOR THE PEOPLE OF YOUGHAL

In a morning filled with silence
        and red clouds,
the bare street leading toward the sea,
moored boats rising with the tide,
hedgerowed hills dark green above the bay,
salmon fishers wrestling the waves,
wives snug in stone shacks,
        I ghost toward the harbor along
worn walls wet with dew.

Ireland's walls run dark and broken
        but the faces of children
color like the morning sky.
Their chattering could be the rooks
        whirling like black confetti
over the town at evening.

The tide slops over my boat like soup.
        Taut lines turn and yaw.
Sole, mottled black and brown,
thump in the stern, turn
        a cloudy eye on me before
the last quivered stiffening.

But I am dumb to fish reproach —
        the popping eye,
the flexing gills —
as are the salmon men
        who pull and haul the tide
with no more effort than the moon.

Icicles of light
            change to diamond fields.
The concave face of a cliff
and its huge shadow
            turn over like a windmill
with cloudy blades.

Flood tide is a stillness of the moon.
            Water makes a world of its own.
At the edge of the Gulf Stream
light lanes curve toward a buoy —
            red with a white stripe —
some whale-child's toy.

I gut the sixteen sole, one bass,
            and beach the boat.
The pailful of fish
set in a recess of the cliff,
            I climb.
My fingers turn to stone.

I think of men whose lives sound like the wind
            whipping along the cliffs,
whose heads
sink as low in stout as the hills in winter fog,
whose words tumble out of their mouths like birds —
cursing the bays and skies,
daydreaming of New York,
            Cousin Liam in Chicago,
two hundred dollars a week.

New Poems

LEAVING IRELAND

Range on range of minor mountains
crease the bay. Continents stand
to port and starboard —
any place and thing imagined
lies waiting to be discovered by the wind.

Tide-drag,
headland-bottleneck,
set spinning on the corkscrewed sea,
horizon distances,
cartography of clouds.

Through bits of stars the tossing foam
lifts to the wind, the daytime blue
ungilded sky begins to glow.
A quietness of wings descends —
the angel stillness of the sea.

Always quick with a long goodbye —
poised, at last, upon the cliff,
hand upraised, the other shading
the nubbin of your face
(an abbreviation

of the Irish race),
body brown as a
withered berry,
but filling the cotton
shift with heat.

Go back to your ikons and praises.
Back to the village dusk
with its rooks and children's cries,
and the hearth that is always flaring,
and the parish of the satisfied.

You wouldn't come.
The wind has freshened,
slapping at the coarsened sails.
You wouldn't come. The dark lies waiting
there at the end of the world.

RETURN

I want to go back to Italy.
I want to sit on the banks of the Arno.
I want to think of the girl who was with me
ten years ago,
and let the memories
(a packet of letters
too long tied up and hidden)
loose on the river
and watch the current pull them away.

I want to know again
the grace of exaggeration
in defiance of reality,
the cheerful lies about everything.
I want to remember the porter
at the *Albergo
Speranza e Commercio*
(the Inn of Hope & Commerce!)
who dragged up five stone flights of steps
an enormous soft bed
to replace the broken cot —
how small he was, and wiry,
and how his brown eyes were as dreamy as a goat's.

I want to let everything loose on the river.
I want to see this body
in the middle of the Arno.
I want it to go one way or the other.
I want to see the ungraven image
dissolve and drain away.
And when I look again at the river —
at the cypresses and willows,
the statue-smooth green flowing —
I shall have become one of those small figures
at the edge of a painting
by a Quattrocento master —
anonymous, a stroke.

OSSABAW SUITE

(for Eleanor Torrey West and Milton Klonsky)

I

Horseshoe crabs snuggle in the muddy
bosom of a tidal creek. Dead oyster
hawsers anchor the island ships.
The full moon tide
froths over Cabbage Garden's lip.
Dented palms,
branches turned like gnarled hands,
rattle at the large
brown toes of live oaks.
Japonicas and tulip trees,
loud two months ago,
leave only the odd azalea tongue
to smear, like lipstick, in the rain.

A tall day's downpour.
A marsh grass mat
of green and brown
steams in and out of distances.
Beyond the rim
of watercolor trees
unstable dunes
point toward the sea
their speckled noses.

A cardinal in a pine tree,
barely visible:
four notes follow each other
like four more birds in flight.

87

A toad's hot belly on the cold red tile,
the skinks and lizards, black and garter snakes
(totems of the poisonous),
the fiddler crabs waving *me! me! me!*
(one claw hitched to the universe,
spider legs halfway down a hole) —
all the unsavory mudhole things
squirming and stalking, humping each other,
in that allegiance to the blood
we have come back to recover.

II

On Half Moon Road there's a black and white
cow with a metronomic tail:
bird notes arc hemidemisemiquavers.

Three large shadows sweep the piney spaces,
that might be poetry's
three graces.

You look up at the half-dark stories
of live oak palaces — the wind
far off as surf —

and think of Antigone,
Sappho, Penelope —
whose traces are footprints

worn in stone
on paths to temples
and temple gardens —

whose great hearts lie,
as these trees' . . .
metrically locked.

III

The wind off the creek is off the sea. . .
The leaf floor looks like peanut brittle
laid in beds of fresh pine needles.
Rapunzel unbraids her greying hair
from every branch;
the live oaks sink
hearts in a swamp.
They ask only that the earth
continue with the sun,
March days drip for days,
and May, like a warm hand,
move from bough to bough.

Let it be revised —
my life laid out
with roots exposed,
moss torn away; I ask —
like a man who has worn a beard
for life
and longs to see his face again —
to be rid of this dream:
the deputy with whom I am riding
the road to the orphans home —
the windshield images
rain fills, and the wiper cleans.

Ossabaw Island, Georgia
May 26, 1976

WAKING UP IN RABUN GAP

(for Mary Nikas)

Willfully awake
or slack asleep and dreaming —
light was looking in
with eyes wide as windows.
Refractions of the glass
struck his face like bits
of mica on the path.
He rolled where the shadows
of leaves swayed on the bed clothes,
and knew that life was love
of things you did not sense —
so small only the light
could tell you they were there —
that we move through days like oxen,
while the delicate air
dances on our feet.

A FABLE

Father clamoured as he came,
and stumbled on the lamp.

Mother sat and waited
for the hard slap —

which, in turn, was not long coming,
though his hands were trembling,

and waving about as though in prayer,
or about to clap.

Father leaped, as from a sheer
cliff, then drew back in a heap,

gathered his long legs beneath him —
struck his hand upon the table.

The moon which like a silver prince
(before he came) adorned the window

descended to an unknown ship
and sailed away, as in a fable.

Lightning and thunder shook
the crockery, and it rattled.

Father lay fatigued in the corner,
a soldier after battle.

Mother's eyes were dry and bright,
and the little crinkles

around them drew within themselves
and left only the wrinkles.

Baby, in the darkened room,
sucked the bottle, and licked the spoon,

then woke against cold breast and side,
and sat up, and peed, and cried.

THE KNOLL

The wind seemed a river underground,
working at roots, like a dark stream —
an echo from the netherworld.

I could feel
the polar reaches, imagine the Arctic
fixed, immutable, whiter

than anything I would ever know,
lying in the grasses, watching clouds,
saying that one was from South Dakota,

the cumulus,
Africa, and the puff
from Tulsa,

forty miles away —
drowsy, dizzied by the sky,
growing with the grass.

REDWOODS

they make such huge shadows
they seem
to drift like clouds

in the fog
they stand so still
you think they're about to fall

their roots
are like the spring
at the head of a long river

they do
not even
know their own names

SANDPIPER

racing through
the surf's
lickspittle foam

the wind
rolls over in the dunegrass
like a horse

a bird — a fluff
tangled in its mane
lost

how many miles
eyes crossed
by stars

domestic now
as porchlights
in isolated towns

SUMMER SKIES

(after reading Robert Ardery's "African Genesis")

That field of stars
could be a page
of dots on which
to draw the night
thousands of years ago:
a leopard's husky cough;
bone of an antelope
shifted in a sweaty hand.

Cursed with prophecy,
and intellectual fear;
by pitfall
and sceptre of bone —
by incidence
of chance, and wilder chance
they gazed on summer skies.

ON THE DEATH OF NERUDA

Out of a vacancy of sky,
out of pure atmosphere,
colorless and unalloyed, the wind
without history or beginning
is all at once here —
shredding the last leaves from limbs,
forcing its presence on everything.
I sometimes think the wind
coming from great distances
(the unsteady seething way
it beats across these fields)
bears the mumblings of confused
millions who have starved
humbly, standing in lines;
that they who were denied
the affections of the times
squat in the rickety
houses of the wind;
that somehow they survive,
heard
but never understood.
We hold our arms,
not from the cold
but out of fear
of the unknown.

THEY

Their eyes, sails the wind has gorged.
Their ears,
spiderwebs.
They are always sitting in the next room
like Whistler's mother.

They have names like George and Mary.
The dogs worn to husks
they take the same seats in buses for years.
And when a child asks why the cane is white
they smile behind their teeth.

BUTTERFLY

He nudges the fish with a spiny toe —
face sunk behind his eyes
like a moon,
eyes anchored on the blue
trembling gills.

He cannot stop
the blood in its mouth
or the almost compassionate grin
that is straining
to fly off his face.

The fish is a friend
who died at sea.
Watching it sink
the fluttering fins
remind him of a butterfly.

WEB IN THE LAMP

Like one of those model airplanes
someone you used to know
suspended from the ceiling —
hung by a film of gauze
so thin only the light
abuts on the length of it,
the moth looks in mid-flight,
wings drawn for another beat.

No story of the struggle —
no image of the spider
hauling up the noose
to hold her victim close;
only a milk-white moth
twists from a single strand,
fixed as though by hand.

ALBA

light   the cold distances
it travels from a star
to bend through slatted blinds
and take the tallest shadows
from the corners of the room

how it stripes the chests
of children   whose small mouths
smell of stale milk
whose hands like voyagers
of the substance and the breath
have swung around like boats
moored in a running tide
whose dreams lie condensed
in sweat above their lips

innocent of death
and of one another
they lie there more alive
today than any other

FOR THE MOTHER OF US ALL

The rain
on the roof
is really not the rain
but a woman
telling a child a story.

That story is a dream
in which we each come true.
The dark side of the moon
of ourselves
turned to view.

The story has no ending
nor any wild surprise.
The dark side of the moon
is any color you can name
in the woman's eyes.

SAIL

from a green tangle
bright as though painted
a bird drifts upward
toward the rain
toward clouds that moil and hiss
like a litter of cats
bird sail
so white, and whiter
like things that leave our lives

THE ANIMALS

Eyes are like animals.
They have their separate bodies.
They have a way
of looking off
and keeping secret what they find.
They see you
in the oddest places
and wonder what you're doing there.
When eyes look into rivers
they do not see themselves
going over and over
the same rocks in the same direction
but know they are like the water
the river will take forever
to carry away.
The best
are like those animals
which come out only at night
when the trees are still, and the river
is carrying the moon downstream.
Then all those closed eyes
are what they were, again.

GODS

the buck recoiled
more than the rubber
butt against your shoulder
the time he took to list
the way his knees touched the ground
the ripeness of his eyes
a moment before they filled with blood
the quiet manner in which he slid
down among the leaves
the vacuum stillness after that
the coolness of what had been hot
my hand upon his neck
we felt that things were not quite right
as though a spirit had been removed
something so huge and wise and gentle
it could have made sense of what we'd done
all we had was a stiff-legged creature
bleeding on the leaves
we felt abandoned by a god

CARNEGIE-MELLON POETRY

The Living and the Dead, Ann Hayes (1975)

In the Face of Descent, T. Alan Broughton (1975)

The Week the Dirigible Came, Jay Meek (1976)

Full of Lust and Good Usage, Stephen Dunn (1976)

How I Escaped from the Labyrinth
and Other Poems, Philip Dacey (1977)

The Lady from the Dark Green Hills, Jim Hall (1977)

For Luck: Poems 1962-1977, H. L. Van Brunt (1977)

By the Wreckmaster's Cottage, Paula Rankin (1977)

108